# THE
# MYSTERY
## OF THE
# GODHEAD

# THE
# MYSTERY
## OF THE
# GODHEAD

## ALBERT SERBIN

XULON PRESS

Xulon Press
2301 Lucien Way #415
Maitland, FL 32751
407.339.4217
www.xulonpress.com

Unless otherwise indicated, Scripture quotations taken
from the King James Version (KJV)–*public domain.*

Paperback ISBN-13: 978-1-66280-029-0

Ebook ISBN-13: 978-1-6628-0030-6

# TABLE OF CONTENTS

**CHAPTER ONE: GODHEAD** . . . . . . . . . . . . . . . . 1

Manifestation
Similitude
Fellow of Jehovah
I AM

**CHAPTER TWO: ONE GOD** . . . . . . . . . . . . . . . . 15

God: Deity, Supreme Being, Divine One
The Supreme One
Jehovah is God
Jehovah is Creator
Jehovah is I AM
Jehovah is the Savior
Jehovah is the Eternal King
Jehovah is the One We Serve
Jehovah is the Lord
Jehovah is the Rock

## CHAPTER THREE: JESUS THE CHRIST ....25

Hidden Name of Yehovah

Greek Word: *Kurios*

The Anointed One—Greek: *Christos*

Jesus is God

Jesus is Creator

Jesus is I AM

Jesus is the Savior

Jesus is the Eternal King

Jesus is Lord

Jesus is the Rock

Unto Us a Child is Born

The Government Shall be upon
His Shoulders

His Name Shall be Called: Wonderful,
Counselor, Mighty God, Everlasting
Father, Prince of Peace

The Humanity of Christ Not Pre-existent—
Declared by the Prophet Isaiah and
the Apostles

The Divinity of Christ Declared by Himself

The Apostles Declare the Divinity of
Christ as God

# CHAPTER FOUR: HOLY SPIRIT. . . . . . . . . . . . 45

Hebrew: *Rauach*

Greek: *Pneuma*

Invisible Force

Symbols of the Spirit: Oil, Fire, Water, Wind

Holy Spirit is Also Known as the Spirit of: Grace, Burning, Truth, Life, Wisdom, Knowledge, Promise, Glory, and Comfort

The Gifts of the Spirit

The Fruits of the Spirit

The Spirit: Omnipotent, Omnipresent, Omniscient

The Sprit in the Old Testament

The Holy Spirit in the New Testament

# INTRODUCTION:

THE MYSTERY OF THE GODHEAD IS ONE OF the most speculative subjects in the Christian world. Throughout history, men with so much knowledge and understanding have drawn conclusions about it from their own hearts. "Likewise, thou son of man, set thy face against the daughters of thy people, which prophecy out of their own heart; and prophecy though against them" (Ezek. 13:17). In the book of Jeremiah, the Word says:

> Therefore, behold, I am against the prophets, saith the LORD that steal my words everyone from his

neighbor. Behold I am against the prophets, saith the LORD, that use their tongues, and say he saith. Behold, I am against them that prophesy false dreams, saith the Lord, and do tell them, and err by their lies, and by their lightness; yet I send them not, nor command them: therefore they shall not profit these people at all, saith the Lord.

- Jeremiah 23:30-32-32

Some say, "God the Father, God the Son, God the Holy Spirit," but in doing so, they are clouded in error because the Bible declares that there is only one God. There has been a battle of the minds in men about this, and the reason is because Satan has watered down the Word of God by injecting lies into truth.

Most of Christianity knows that God chose the Hebrew nation as His witnesses, as stated in Isaiah 43:10: "Ye are my witnesses, saith the LORD, and my servant whom I have chosen: that ye may know and believe me and understand that

I am He: before me there was no God formed, neither shall there be after me." The Hebrew nation has the first principle correct—one God; unfortunately, the Jewish people are clouded in error because they have not accepted Jesus Christ as the Messiah. It is now the church's responsibility to declare the name of the Lord, our righteousness. "To the intent that now unto thee principalities and powers in heavenly places might be known by the church the manifold **wisdom of God**, according to the eternal purpose which he proposed in Christ Jesus our Lord" (Eph. 3:10-11). How can the church fulfill its destiny if it is led by erroneous doctrine of lying spirits and not the Holy Ghost? Therefore, in order to understand the Godhead, we will consult the oracles of God, or the Word of God. The Bible, which is inspired by God, is the only book that can make the claim as being from Him.

God has created, according to His majestic power as recorded by Paul in 1 Corinthians 15:40, celestial bodies and terrestrial bodies, one to abide in the heavenly realm and the other in the earthly realm. Each has its own glory; that is what is glorious about our God. In the beginning,

He was the Word, and the Word became flesh (John 1:1, 14). Jesus transformed from His celestial body to a human body, the only begotten Son, in order to be the Lamb slain from the foundation of the world. Christ would be the ultimate sacrifice from mankind, as stated in Isaiah 53.

This book has been written from sermons, lectures, and personal study from the King James Version. Spanning a period of four decades, all scriptures quoted are from the King James Bible.

# CHAPTER ONE

# THE GODHEAD

Beware lest any man spoil you through philosophy, and vain deceit, after the traditions of man, after the rudiments of the world, and not after Christ. For in Him **dwelleth all the fullness of the Godhead bodily.** And ye are complete in Him, which is the head of all principality and power: I whom also are circumcised with the circumcision made without hands, in putting off the body with Him in baptism, where in

also ye are risen with Him through
the faith of the operation of God,
who had raised Him from the dead.

- Colossians 2:8-13

PAUL WRITING TO THE SAINTS AND
faithful brethren in Christ, who were at Colosse,
made this great statement. He was concerned
about the problems the Colossians were experi-
encing. In this book, he wrote about the freedom
of the law, the outward forms of religion, and
rituals in human philosophies, much the same
way these things are happening today. There are
points of interest in these scriptures which will
be discussed throughout this book. The main
point is that in Christ dwelleth all the fullness
of the Godhead bodily—meaning, Christ is the
one here with a physical body that embraces the
Father and Holy Spirit. Other scriptures to consider in the Godhead are as follows:

For the invisible things of Him from
the creation of the world are clearly
seen, understood by the things

that are made, even His eternal
power and Godhead; so that they
are without excuse: because that,
when they knew God, they glorified Him not as God. Neither were
thankful; but became vain in their
imaginations, and their foolish
hearts were darkened.

- Romans 1:20-21

Paul, in this letter to the church of Rome,
clearly made a profound statement about the
Godhead. As we continue to rightly divide the
Word, we will be enlightened. "And without
controversy great is the mystery of godliness;
(Greek *eusebeia* – reverence toward God; piety)
God was manifested in the flesh, justified in the
Spirit, seen of angels, preached unto the Gentiles,
believed on in the world, received on into glory"
(1 Tim. 3:16). When we acknowledge Jesus
Christ as the true and only God, we are giving
Him the godliness in reverence.

"And we know that the son of God has come,
and hath given us an <u>understanding</u>, that we

may know Him that is true, and we are in Him that is true, even in His son Jesus Christ. This the true God, and eternal life" (1 John 5:20).

In Jewish thought, a name was never a random combination of sounds. A name was meant to convey the nature, essence, history and reputation of a person. The Greek word *Iesous* is a transliteration of the Hebrew *Yeshua*, which means salvation.

Dear reader, how is your knowledge of God, Jesus Christ, and the Holy Ghost? Ask yourself if knowledge about who and what you believe in is important to you. Ask your pastor or spiritual leader about the Godhead and how important it is to understand it. Most people would probably say, "I have not read or studied the subject," and ask, "Is it important?"

> Not everyone that saith unto Me, Lord, Lord, shall enter into the Kingdom of heaven: but he that doeth the will of my Father which is in heaven. Many will say to me in that day, Lord, Lord, have we not prophesied in thy name? And

in thy name case out devils? And in thy name done many wonderful works? And then will I profess unto them, I never knew you: depart from me, ye that work iniquity.

- Matthew 7:21-23

The will of God is to obey the gospel of Jesus Christ. "But let him that glorieth glory in this, that he **understandeth** and **knoweth** me, that I am the LORD which exercise loving kindness, judgment, and righteousness, in the earth: for in these things I delight, saith the LORD" (Jer. 9:24).

"Hear the word of the LORD, ye children of Israel: for the LORD had a controversy with the inhabitants of the land, because there is not truth, nor mercy, nor knowledge of God in the land" (Hos. 4:1).

"My people are destroyed for the lack of knowledge: because thou hast rejected knowledge, I will also reject thee, that they shall be no more priests to me; seen thou hast forgotten the law of thy God. I will also forget thy children" (Hos. 4:6).

"Oh the depths of the riches, both of wisdom and knowledge: how unsearchable are his judgments and his ways finding out" (Rom. 11:3).

"Thus saith the Lord God; woe to the foolish prophets, that follow their own spirit, and have seen nothing" (Ezek. 13:3).

Look around you! In Christianity today, are preachers speaking out of their own foolish hearts? Do they have a firm foundation on the Word of God? The Word says in 1 Corinthians 12:8 and 14:26 that the Holy Spirit will give wisdom, knowledge, and revelation. In Matthew 5:17-18 the Lord said, "I have come to fulfill the law not to do away with it." Without any further ado, let me point out something relevant to this study—celestial bodies:

1. MANIFESTATION: The appearance in bodily form of spirit. "God is a Spirit: and they that worship Him must worship Him in spirit and in truth" (John 4:24). There is a noumenon as Immanuel Kant says in critique of pure reasonam. There is also a noumenon, substrate, or ground behind the manifestation. In each context, one

must determine is the ground behind the manifestation of in simplifies language one must determine what was manifested. Example: 1 Timothy 3:16.

2. SIMILITUDE: Likeness, an image or visible resemblance. "And    it is yet far more evident: for that the similitude of Melchisedec there ariseth another priest, who is not after the law of a carnal commandment but after the power and the endless life" (Heb. 7:15-16). "For whom He did **foreknow**, He also did predestinate to be conformed to the image of His son, that He might be the firstborn among many brethren" (Rom. 8:29). In the plan of God, He knew what the Son would look like. As He said in Genesis 1:26, "Let's make man in our image, a visible resemblance of the invisible God."

"In whom the god of this world, has blinded the mind of them that believe not, lest the light of the glorious gospel of Christ, who is the image of God should shine unto them" (2 Cor. 4:4).

"Who is the image of the invisible God, the first of every creature" (Col. 1:15).

"Who being the brightness of His glory, and the express image of His person, and upholding all things by the word of His power, when He had by Himself purged our sins, sat down on the right hand of the majesty on high" (Heb. 1:3). The Greek word used here—*hupostasis*—is for a person, which is a bad translation because God is a spirit and invisible. Here it refers to the essential substance of God.

"Behold my hand and my feet, that it is I myself: handle me, and see; for a spirit had not flesh and bones, as ye see me have" (Luke 24:39).

"Awake, oh sword, against y shepherd, and against the man that is my fellow, saith the LORD of hosts: smite the shepherd, and the sheep shall be scattered: and I will turn my hand upon the little ones" (Zech. 13:7). Fellow—The Hebrew for fellow, *awmeeth*, has the primitive root meaning of another fellow of the same kind and nature. Jesus Christ had a dual nature, one divine and one human.

Throughout the Old Testament are scriptures that give testimony of the manifestations of God in bodily form. Known to Hebrew scholars for many generations, God's presence was revealed in different forms, dreams, and visions. Shekinah, theophanies, the angel of the Lord—God appearing as a human being. "But though, Bethlehem Ephratah, thou be little among the thousands of Judea, yet, out of thee shall he come forth unto me, that is to be ruler in Israel whose going forth have been from old, from everlasting" (Micah 5:2). Who was this traveler? Whose going forth had been from old, from everlasting? This prophecy was about the birth of Christ, yet He visited earth on a number of occasions and appeared unto men. Let there be no mistake—Jehovah of the Old Testament is Jesus Christ of the New Testament. Let us unfold the mystery of the Godhead in the light of the Word of God.

In the gospel of Matthew, we have the combined unity of divinity and humanity of God and Christ. By the power of God, He was able as the Word using a celestial body. The Word is the divinity of Christ, the invisible substance of the essence that defines God. The most impressive appearances of Jehovah God as a human being are recorded in the books of Genesis and Exodus. "And he lifted up his eyes and looked, and lo three men stood by him; and when he saw them he ran to meet them from the tent door, and bowed himself to the ground" (Gen. 18:2). Here we have clear evidence that God appeared to Abram and Abram bowed before Him. In any other scripture, an angel would forbid a man to kneel before him.

Another example is in Genesis 26:24: "And the LORD appeared unto him that same night, and said, I AM the God of Abraham thy father: fear not, for I AM with thee, and will bless thee, and multiply thy seed for my servant Abraham sake." God was making an appearance to Isaac to confirm the covenant He made with Abraham of a great nation:

> And Jacob was left alone: and there wrestled a man with him until the breaking of the day. And when he saw that he prevailed not against him, he touched the hollow of his thigh: and the hollow of Jacob's thigh was out of joint, as he wrestled with him. And he said, let me go, for the day breaketh. And he said, I will not let thee go, except

thou bless me. And he said unto him, what is thy name? And he said Jacob. And he said, thy name shall be called no more Jacob, but Israel: for as a prince hast thou power with God with men, and has prevailed. And Jacob asked him, and said, tell me, I pray thee, thy name. And he said, where fore is that thou dost ask after my name? And he blessed him there. And Jacob called the place Peniel: for I have seen God face to face, and my life is preserved.

- Genesis 32:24-30

Jacob called the place Peniel, meaning "face of God," and his life was preserved. The above scriptures of the appearance of God are special, His going forth throughout history. They reveal as we have stated before that God is a Spirit but can also appear as a man. That is the power of almighty God—transforming a celestial body to a terrestrial body by the power of His word (spoken word) which existed with Him, a celestial body that could materialize at His command.

In the book of Exodus, almighty God revealed His name to Moses:

> And the angel of the LORD appeared unto him in a flame of fire out of the mist of a bush: and he locked, and, behold the bush burned with fire, and the bush was not consumed. And God said unto Moses, I AM THAT I AM: and He said, thus shalt thou say unto the children of Israel, I AM hath sent me unto you. And God said moreover unto Moses, thus shalt thou say unto the children of Israel, the LORD God of your fathers, the God of Abraham, the God of Isaac, and the God of Jacob, hath sent me unto you: this is my name forever, and this is my memorial unto all generations.
>
> - Exodus 3:2, 14-15

"And I appeared unto Abraham, unto Isaac, and unto Jacob, by the name of God almighty, but by my name Jehovah was I not known to them" (Ex. 6:3).

In both of these passages, God made a powerful statement about His name to Moses. First of all, it was a revelation of who He was. This is His name forever, a memorial to all generations from the time of Moses to the second coming of the LORD. His name is Yehovah in the Old Testament and Yeshua in the New Testament.

CHAPTER TWO

# ONE GOD

---

SINCE THE CREATION OF MAN, HE HAS always wanted to know who God is and how He came into existence. Man, of course, has had a limited knowledge of God and therefore a speculative understanding. The man who has a true experience with God, however, should know his God. And this experience will be supernatural for God is a spirit.

The best source about God is the Bible. Many religions are based on the same documents (the Bible) but have brought out their own twisted doctrines and philosophies. The oracles of God, according to Paul in 2 Timothy 3:16 states, "All scripture is given by inspiration of God and is profitable for doctrine, for reprove, for correction, for instruction in all righteousness."

The Bible reveals the mind of God for it was God's spirit that made great revelations to man. The Bible contains God's interaction with man and the history of man's past, present, and future existence with or without God.

Definition of the word God—God is the common appellation in the Bible for deity, divine nature, divine substance, the one divine essence. Therefore, when I talk about the one divine nature, the one divine substance, or the one divine essence, I am referring to the one true God.

- God: Deity, Supreme Being, Divine One.
- Elohim (plural of Elohim—gods): The Supreme God, Creator. Elohim indicates the relation to man as Creator and is in contrast with Yehovah, which indicates He is in a covenant relationship with creation.
- Yehovah: Self-existent of eternal one. Lord, the Jewish national name of God, when

translated is Adonai, Yehovah, Lord God.
(Gen. 15:28; Deut. 3:24, 9:26; Josh. 2:7).
- El: Strength. El is the strong and mighty
one, the Almighty, the Most High God.
- Elohah: Deity, God the Divine One—found
only in Ezra 4:24. Rock, Refuge (Isa. 44:8).

One main Greek word of God is *Theos*,
meaning "deity."

**THE SUPREME ONE:**

No one religion on earth can claim its god is
the only true god, except for the God of Israel,
because God has revealed Himself since creation and throughout history—first to Adam and
then to Moses, who is credited with the first five
books of the Bible. "Hear, O Israel: The LORD our
God is one God" (Deut. 6:4).

Man has lived much like he wants, without
God. From the time of Adam to Abraham, men
lived according to their conscience—at times,
including God in their lives and paying tribute
to Him, and other times, without God and with
no moral liability. I would like to believe that

Adam told his sons and that his sons told their sons about God in order to keep the memorial of God alive.

The cradle of civilization is centered at Mesopotamia. There existed a civilization known as the Chaldeans. According to history, these people were intelligent and were also recorded in the Old Testament. They lived in the southern part of Babylon, which today would be the southern part of Iraq. Abraham was called out from this pagan land whose god was the moon. God has always chosen people who will listen to His word and obey it.

"Now the LORD (Yehovah) had said unto Abram, Get thee out of thy country, and from thy kindred, and from thy father's house, unto a land that I will shew thee" (Gen. 12:1). In Genesis 12:8, we find Abram building an altar unto the Lord and calling upon His name. How did Abram know to build an altar? Perhaps from his fathers all the way back to Noah for Noah also built an altar after the flood. Note: "And called upon the name of the Lord," means that Abram "invoked" the Lord's name—called it out, pronouncing it.

We know the history as recorded in Genesis and Exodus how God used Moses to deliver His people and gave him the law by which they should live and honor God.

"Know therefore this day, and consider it in thy heart that the LORD He is God in heaven above and upon the earth and beneath; there is none else" (Deut. 4:39).

"See now that I, even I, am He and there is no god with me: I kill, and make alive; I wound and heal; neither is there any that can deliver out of my hand" (Deut. 32:39).

"Ye are my witnesses, saith the LORD, and my servant whom I have chosen that ye may know and believe me and understand that I AM He: before me there was no god formed, neither shall there be after Me. I, even I, am the LORD; and beside Me there is no Savior" (Isa. 43:10-11).

"Tell ye, and bring them near; yea, let them take counsel together: who hath declared this from ancient time? Who hath told it from that time? Have not I the LORD? And there is no god beside Me; a just God and Savior; there is none beside Me" (Isa. 45:21-22).

"Remember the former things of old; for I am God, and there is none else; I AM God, and there is none like me" (Isa. 46:9).

There is no confusion in the Word of God and no room for personal interpretations or opinions. There is only one God. So how could Jesus make the same claim? Look beyond the human mind and see the spiritual revelation. Some of the scriptures have already been included, but I repeat them to stress the point of interest.

## YEHOVAH IS GOD:

"The LORD GOD of your fathers" (Ex. 3:15).
"By my name Yehovah was I not known" (Ex. 6:3).
"Is there a god besides Me? Yea, there is no god; I know not of any" (Isa. 44:8).
"I am the LORD, and there is none else" (Isa. 45:6).

## YEHOVAH IS CREATOR:

"And the LORD God planed a garden eastward in Eden" (Gen. 2:8).

"I am the LORD that maketh all things" (Isa. 44:24).

## YEHOVAH IS THE I AM:

"And God said unto Moses, I AM THAT I AM" (Ex. 3:14).

## YEHOVAH IS THE SAVIOR:

"I, even I, AM the LORD; and beside me there is no savior" (Isa. 43:11).

## YEHOVAH IS THE ETERNAL KING:

"Thou art my king, O God; command deliverance for Jacob" (Ps. 44:4).

"With trumpets and sound of cornet make a joyful noise before the LORD, the King" (Ps. 98:6).

"Thus saith the LORD the King of Israel" (Isa. 44:6).

"But the LORD is the true God, He is the living God, and the everlasting King" (Jer. 10:10).

"As I live, saith the King, whose name is the LORD of hosts" (Jer. 46:18).

## YEHOVAH IS THE ONE WE SERVE:

"To love the LORD your God, and to serve Him with all your heart and with all your soul" (Deut. 6:13).

"Know therefore fear the LORD, and serve in sincerity and in truth. And if it seem evil unto you to serve the LORD, choose you this day whom ye will serve" (Josh. 24:14-15).

## YEHOVAH IS THE LORD:

"Hear O Israel: The LORD our God is one LORD" (Deut. 6:4).

## YEHOVAH IS THE ROCK:

"There is none holy as the LORD: for there is none beside thee: neither is there any rock like our God" (1 Sam. 2:2).

"For who is God, save the LORD? And who is a rock, save our God?" (1 Sam. 22:32).

NOTE: Wherever LORD is written in capital letters, it means Yehovah, the name of God.

The scriptures above speak in plain language about Yehovah and give testament that Yehovah is God.

"O, LORD, there is none like thee, neither is there any god beside according to all that we have heard with our ears" (1 Chron. 17:20).

"The secret things belong unto the LORD our God: but those things which are revealed belong to us and to our children forever, that we may do all the words of the law" (Deut. 29:29).

Remember the scripture where the Lord said, "I have come to fulfill the law, not to do away with the law" (Matt. 5:17-18)? The law is now written in our hearts. Throughout the Old Testament, Yehovah God stated that He was the only GOD. Later on in the Word, we see that Jesus Christ made the same claims.

CHAPTER THREE

# JESUS THE CHRIST

YEHOVAH IS HIDDEN IN THE NAME OF Jesus. In reality, when we say Jesus (Yeshua), we are saying Yehovah is with us or Yehovah the Savior. The English name Jesus is translated from the Greek (Isoues), which comes from the Hebrew, Yehovah. The name of Jesus Christ covers both divinity and humanity, both before the incarnation of God in the flesh after, when God added immortal man to the Godhead.

"That if thou shalt confess with thy mouth the Lord Jesus, and shall believe in thy heart that God had raised him from the dead, thou shalt be saved" (Rom. 10:9). Paul used the Greek word *Kuros* for the Lord in this scripture, which is the same word used in Joel 2:32 for Yehovah. This word was used to represent both God and Christ and translated as "Lord" 669 times, equivalent to the use of Yehovah in the Old Testament. There can only be one Yehovah, even though some may think there are two by these statements.

"In the beginning was the word, and the word was with God, and the word was God [The same was in the beginning with God]...And the word was made flesh, and dwelt among us (and we beheld His glory, the glory as in the begotten of the Father,) full of grace and truth" (John 1:1-2, 14). The Word in the Old Testament, to the Hebrew mind, stood for power. "He sent forth His word and healed them" (Ps. 107:20).

The Word also stood for God's wisdom: "the Lord possessed me in the beginning of His way, before His works of old" (Prov. 8:22). The name Jesus means God is salvation. Therefore, His name is not of human origin but of heavenly origin. Yehovah revealed His name; therefore, this name should be exalted—Yehovah is the Savior of mankind. Cristos is the Greek form of

Christ, meaning the anointed one. It is important to unite the name of Jesus and Christ, thus Jesus Christ. Peter did this in Acts 2:38. The union of names completes the unity of God and man; one is divine, and the other is human. After the resurrection of Jesus Christ, He put on immortality, a glorified body.

> Wherefore God also hath exalted Him, and given Him a name which is above every name: that at the name of Jesus every knee should bow, that things in heaven, in earth, and the things under the earth; and that every tongue should confess that Jesus Christ is Lord, to the Glory of God the Father.
>
> - Philippians 2:9-11

It is evident that no name could be higher than the Father's name. God gave Jesus His own name. "Behold a virgin shall be with child, and shall bring forth a son, and they shall call His name

Emmanuel, which being interpreted is, God with us" (Matt. 1:23).

"And behold, thou shalt conceive in thy womb, and bring forth a son, and shall call His name JESUS" (Luke 1:31).

"Being made so much better than angels, as He by inheritance obtained a more excellent name than they" (Heb. 1:4).

"Jesus said unto them, verily I say unto you. Before Abraham was I am" (John 8:58). In truth, Jesus was telling the Pharisees that He was Yehovah. Earlier, He said, "I am come in my Father's name" (John 5:43), rightly so for He received His excellent name by inheritance. Let there be no mistake that the evidence presented by Scripture gives testimony that Yehovah of the Old Testament is Yeshua in the New Testament.

> For the wrath of God is revealed from heaven against all ungodliness and unrighteousness of man, who hold the truth in unrighteousness; because that which may be known of God is manifested in them for God has showed it unto

them. For the invisible things of Him for the creation of the world are clearly seen, being understood by the things that are made, even His eternal power and Godhead; so that they are without excuse: because that, when they knew God, they Glorified Him not as God, neither were thankful; but became vain in their imaginations, and their foolish heart was darkened. Professing themselves to be wise, they became fools, and changed the glory of the un-corruptible God into an image made like a corruptible man, and to birds, and to four footed beasts, land creeping things. Wherefore also God gave them up to the uncleanness through the lust of their own hearts, to dishonor their own bodies between themselves: changed the truth of God to a lie, and served the creature more than the creator, who is blessed forever. Amen.

- Romans 1:18-25

One of the greatest mysteries of the Bible is how God hid His majesty and power behind the veil of flesh. "By a new and living way, which He had consecrated for us. Through the veil, that is to say His flesh" (Heb. 10:20). The Jewish nation is blind of this profound mystery, in spite of the fact that so many prophesies of the Messiah in the Old Testament point to Jesus Christ. Most of the Christian world is also blind because of false doctrines, therefore clouded in error. One must be careful with the Word of God and not let seducing spirits cloud our minds in error, as Paul was so ready to point out. "Now the spirit expressly, that in the latter times some shall depart from the faith, giving heed to seducing spirits, and doctrines of devils; speaking lies in hypocrisy; having their conscience seared with a hot iron" (1 Tim. 4:1-2).

Consider the following and compare to the Old Testament Yehovah: Jesus is God, Jesus is

Creator, Jesus is the I AM, Jesus is the Savior, Jesus is the eternal King, Jesus is the one we serve, Jesus is the Lord, and Jesus is the rock.

## JESUS IS GOD:

"The mighty God" (Isa. 9:6).

"And Thomas answered and said unto Him, my LORD and my God" (John 20:28).

"God was manifested in the flesh" (1 Tim. 3:16).

"Looking for that blessed hope, and the glorious appearing of the great God and our savior Jesus Christ" (Titus 2:13).

## JESUS IS CREATOR:

"He was in the world, and the world was made by Him, and he world knew Him not" (John 1:10).

"And unto the angel of the church in Smyrna write; these things saith the first and the last, which was dead is alive" (Rev. 2:8).

## JESUS IS THE I AM:

"I am alpha and omega, the beginning and the end, the first and the last" (Rev. 22:13).

"Jesus said unto them verily, verily I say unto you, before Abraham was, I am" (John 8:58).

## JESUS IS THE SAVIOR:

"For unto you is born this day in the city of David a Savior, which is Christ the Lord" (Luke 2:11). Also reference Titus 2:13.

"But grown in grace, and in the knowledge of our Lord and savior Jesus Christ" (2 Peter 3:18).

"To the only wise God our Savior, be gory and majesty, dominion and power, both now and for-ever amen" (Jude 25).

## JESUS IS THE ETERNAL KING:

"Thou sayest that I am king. To this end was I born, and for this cause came I unto the world, that I should bear witness unto the truth. Everyone that is of the truth heareth my voice" (John 18:37).

"Which in His times He shall shew, who is the blessed and only potentate, the Kings of kings, and Lord of lords" (1 Tim. 6:15).

"For He is Lord of lords, and King of kings" (Rev. 17:14).

"And He had on His vesture and on His thigh a name written, KING of KINGS and LORD of LORDS" (Rev. 19:16).

## JESUS IS THE ONE WE SERVE:

"If any man serve me, let him follow me; and where I am, there shall also my servant be: if any man serve me, him will my father honor" (John 12:26).

"For he that is called in the Lord, being a servant, is the Lord's free man: likewise also he that is called, being free, is Christ's servant" (1 Cor. 7:22).

"Knowing that the Lord ye shall receive the reward of the inheritance: for ye serve the Lord Christ" (Col. 3:24).

## JESUS IS THE LORD:

"For unto you is born this day in the city of David a Savior, which is Christ the Lord" (Luke 2:11).

"Therefore let all the house of Israel know assuredly, that God hath made that same Jesus, whom you have crucified, both Lord and Christ" (Acts 2:36).

"And he said, who art thou, Lord? And the Lord said, I am Jesus whom thou persecutest: it is hard for thee to kick against the pricks" (Acts 9:5).

"But to us there is but one God, the Father, of whom are all things, and we in Him; and one Lord Jesus Christ, by whom are all things, and we by Him" (1 Cor. 8:6).

## JESUS IS THE ROCK:

The Greek word used was *peta*, meaning an immovable stone.

"The stone which the builders refused is become the headstone of the corner" (Ps. 118:22).

"Therefore thus saith the Lord God, behold, I lay in Zion for a foundation, a tried stone, a precious corner stone, a sure foundation: he that believeth shall not make haste" (Isa. 28:16).

"For the foundation can no man lay than that is laid, which is Jesus Christ" (1 Cor. 3:11).

"And did all drink the same spiritual drink: or they drank of that spiritual rock that followed them: and that rock was Christ" (1 Cor. 10:4).

"And are built upon the foundation of the apostles and prophets, Jesus Christ himself being the chief corner stone" (Eph. 3:20).

"And I say also unto thee, that thou art Peter, and upon this rock I will build my church: and the gates of hell shall not prevail against it" (Matt. 16:18).

NOTE: When Jesus was speaking to Peter, it was an allegory meaning of Himself, the central meaning that Jesus was the rock as provided by the above scriptures.

"For unto us a child is born, unto us a child is given: and the government shall be upon his shoulder: and his name shall be called wonderful, counselor, the might God, the Everlasting Father and the prince of peace" (Isa. 9:6).

NOTE: The Hebrew for God (Elohim) is used most frequently in plural form.

## UNTO US A CHILD IS BORN:

"And she shall bring forth a son, and thou shall call his name JESUS: for he shall save his people from their sins" (Matt. 1:21).

"Behold, a virgin shall be with child, and shall bring forth a son, and they shall call his name Emmanuel, which being interpreted is, God with us" (Matt. 1:23).

"But when the fullness of the times was come, God sent forth His son, made woman, made under the law, to redeem them that were under the law, that we might receive the adoption of sons" (Gal. 4:4-5).

## UNTO US A CHILD IS GIVEN:

"For God so loved the world, that he gave his only begotten son. That who so ever believeth in him shall not perish, but have everlasting life" (John 2:16).

## THE GOVERNMENT SHALL BE UPON HIS SHOULDERS:

NOTE: The Hebrew word is *misrah,* which means empire, government.

"All power is given unto me in heaven and in earth" (Matt. 2:18).

"For he has been highly exalted far above all principality, and power, and might, and dominion, and every name that is named" (Eph. 1:20).

## HIS NAME SHALL BE CALLED WONDERFUL:

NOTE: Wonderful in Hebrew is *pele*, meaning a miracle, wonder. One of the most wonderful miracles recorded in the Scriptures is the virgin birth of Jesus Christ (Matt. 1:21-23).

"And the angel of the Lord said unto him. Why askest thou thus after my name, seeing that it is secret? So Manoah took a kid with meat offering, and offered it upon a rock unto the Lord: and the angel did wonderously: and Manoah and his wife looked on" (Judg. 13:18-19).

## COUNSELOR:

"And I will pray the Father, and he shall give you another comforter, that he may abide with you forever; even the spirit of truth; whom the word cannot receive, because it seeth him not, neither knoweth him: but ye know him; for he dwelleth with you, and shall be in you" (John 14:16-17).

## MIGHTY GOD:

NOTE: The Hebrew word is *gibbor*, meaning powerful, almighty.

"And I appeared unto Abraham, unto Isaac, and unto Jacob by the name of God almighty" (Ex. 6:3).

"And now, O Father, glorify thou me with thy own self with the glory that I had with thee before the world was" (John 17:5).

## EVERLASTING FATHER:

"One God and Father of all who is above all, and through all, and in all" (Eph. 4:6).

## THE PRINCE OF PEACE:

"And he shall judge among the nations, and shall rebuke many people: and they shall bent their swords into plow sheers, and their spears into pruning hooks: nation shall not life sword against nation, neither shall they learn war anymore" (Isa. 2:6).

When one begins to write on the subject of Jesus Christ, one hardly knows if he is giving complete honor to our Lord and Savior. It is the greatest subject that has been brought to the attention of men. Men in all ages were confused as to His deity. Many books have been written about Him, but only the Scriptures give Him the honor He is due. Multitudes use His name as a curse on their lips, but only a small amount of people truly know and understand Him. In Romans, Paul spoke about the gospel of Christ as the ultimate plan of salvation. "Because that, when they knew God, they glorified him not as God, neither were thankful; but became vain in their imaginations, and their foolish heart was darkened" (Rom. 1:21).

## THE HUMANITY OF CHRIST NOT PRE-EXISTENT:

The reader should not confuse the humanity of Christ with the pre-existence of Christ. It has been revealed through Scripture that it was the divinity of Christ that pre-existed. "For verily he took not on him the nature of angels; but he took on the seed of Abraham" (Heb. 2:16). The Word was spoken by God and sent forth. Christ was both God and man, divinity and humanity united. "For there are three that bear record in heaven, the Father the Word, and the Holy Ghost: and these three are one" (1 John 5:7). Notice that the Son was not mentioned in this record for it is a heavenly record. Christ is the glorified Word. Consider this line of reasoning—since the whole Word of God was established in the Old Testament, there is only one God. The union of two perfect natures, divinity and humanity, qualify Christ to be the mediator, His shed blood a reconciliation between them. "To wit, that God was in Christ reconciling the world until himself" (2 Cor. 5:19). "No man cometh unto the Father, but by me" (John 14:16).

## THE DIVINITY OF JESUS CHRIST DECLARES HIM AS GOD:

Jesus said: "Before Abraham was I AM" (John 8:58).

Jesus said: "I and my Father are one" (John 10:30).

Jesus said: "Believe that the Father is in me, and I in him" (John 10:32).

Jesus said: "He that hath seen me, hath seen the Father" (John 14:9).

Jesus said: "Believe me that I am n the Father, and the Father in me" (John 14:11).

Jesus said: "At that day ye shall know that I am in my Father, and ye in me, and I in you" (John 14:20).

"I am alpha and omega, the beginning and the ending...the Almighty" (Rev. 1:8).

"I am the first and the last" (Rev. 1:17).

## THE APOSTLES DECLARE THE DIVINITY OF CHRIST AS GOD:

"In the beginning was the word, and the word was with God, and the word was God...And the word was made flesh and dwelt among us" (John 1:1-2, 14).

Thomas said: "My Lord and my God" (John 20:28).

John said that Jesus Christ, "Is the true God and eternal life" (1 John 5:20).

Paul said Christ was: "God blessed forever" (Rom. 9:6).

Paul said: "Thy throne, O God, is forever and ever" (Heb. 1:8).

Paul said: "God was manifest in the flesh" (1 Tim. 3:16).

Jude said: "Only wise God" (25).

## THE PROPHET DECLARES THE HUMANITY OF CHRIST:

He was a man of sorrows, one acquainted with grief, with no form of comeliness, And no beauty in him that we should desire him, he was wounded; he was bruised; he was stripped and on him was laid the iniquity of us all. He was oppressed; he was afflicted; he was taken from prison and judgement. He was cut off from the land of the living; he was stricken; he made his grave with the wicked, and with the rich in his death.

- Isaiah 53:5-9

## THE APOSTLES DECLARE THE HUMANITY OF CHRIST:

Peter said that Jesus was, "A man approved of God" (Acts 2:22).

Paul said: "He will judge the world in righteousness by that man" (Acts 17:31).

Paul said: "Gift by grace is by one man, Jesus Christ" (Rom. 5:15).

Paul said: "By man came also the resurrections of the dead" (1 Cor. 15:21).

Paul said: "One mediator between God and men, the man Christ Jesus" (1 Tim. 2:5).

CHAPTER FOUR

# THE HOLY SPIRIT, HOLY GHOST

THE SCRIPTURES CONCERNING THE HOLY
Spirit would lack harmony outside of the fact or
truth that Christ is both God and man. The mar-
velous fact of the dual nature of Christ brings
them into perfect harmony. There is a general
belief that the Godhead consists of three sepa-
rated persons; therefore many refer to the Holy
Spirit as the third person in the Holy Trinity. The
Bible does not use the word person when referring to the Holy Spirit. In fact, the word person
is from the word mask. This mask was worn by
actors to portray a character. According to *The*

*Living Webster Encyclopedic Dictionary of the English Language* (page 708), the word person is applied to human beings—man, woman, or child.

The Hebrew word for spirit is *rauach*, in the Greek *pneuma*. The primary meaning of both is invisible force. Man in his natural state of mind, carnal (spiritual blindness), seeks to speculate ideas of God's Spirit. Man has many speculations, which has resulted in so many twisted and unbiblical doctrines. He has adopted the word person and applied it to the Godhead. In the study of the Scriptures, there is one God, and this one true God has manifested Himself as Father in creation, Son in redemption, and Holy Spirit in justification. There is no controversy in the oracles of God concerning the Spirit for there is only one Spirit. "There is one body, and one Spirit, even as ye are called in one hope of your calling; one Lord, one faith, and one baptism" (Eph. 4:4).

Scripture in the Old Testament referring to the Spirit of God also referred to the Holy Spirit in the New Testament. "But ye are not in the flesh, but in the Spirit, if so be that the Spirit of

God dwell in you. Now if any man have not the Spirit of Christ, he is none of his" (Rom. 8:9).

There are symbols used in speaking of the Spirit—oil, fire, water, and wind. The Holy Spirit is also known as the Spirit of grace (Heb. 10:29), the Spirit of burning (Matt. 3:11-12; Isa. 4:4), the Spirit of truth (John 14:17, 15:26, 16:13; 1 John 5:6), the Spirit of wisdom and knowledge (Isa. 11:2, 61:1-2; Luke 4:18), the Spirit of promise (Eph. 1:3), the Spirit of glory (1 Peter 4:14), and the Comforter (John 14:16-17).

The Holy Spirit also has fruits, which are recorded in Galatians 5:22. The Spirit is omnipotent (Luke 1:35), omnipresent (Ps. 139:7-10), and omniscient (1 Cor. 2:10 -11).

The apostles were instructed to go to Jerusalem and wait until they were endowed with power (Luke 24:49). This power would include the gifts and fruits of the Spirit. The gifts of the Spirit are words of wisdom, words of knowledge, faith, healings, working of miracles, prophecy, discerning of spirits, diverse kinds of tongues, and interpretation of tongues (1 Cor. 12:1, 7-10).

"But the natural man receveth not the things of the Spirit of God: for they are foolishness unto him: neither can he know them, because they are spiritually discerned" (1 Cor. 2:14). This scripture is so true. There are people who call themselves Christians today who do not even believe in the Holy Spirit. "And it shall come to pass afterward, that I will pour out of my Spirit upon all flesh; and you sons and your daughters shall prophesy, and your old men shall dream dreams, you young men shall see visions" (Joel 2:28).

## HOLY SPIRIT IN THE OLD TESTAMENT:

"And the earth was without form, and bold; and darkness was upon the face of the deep and the Spirit of God moved upon the face of the waters" (Gen. 1:2).

"Pharaoh said unto his servants concerning Joseph: can we find such one as this is: a man in whom the Spirit of God is" (Gen. 41:38).

"And he had filled him with the Spirit of God, in wisdom, in understanding, and in knowledge, and in all manner of workmanship" (Ex. 35:31).

"And I will come down and talk with thee there: and I will take of the spirit which is upon thee: and will put it upon them; and they shall bear the burden of the people with thee, that thou bear it not thyself alone" (Num. 11:17).

"And Balaam lifted up his eyes, and he saw Israel abiding in his tents according to their tribes; and the Spirit of God came upon him" (Num. 24:2).

"And the Spirit of the Lord came upon him and he judged Israel" (Judg. 3:10).

"But the Spirit of the Lord came upon Gideon, and he blew a trumpet; Abiezer was gathered after him" (Judg. 6:34).

"Then the Spirit of the Lord came upon Jephthan, and he passed over Gilead, and Manasseh, and passed over Mizpeh of Gilead, and from Mispeht of Gilead he passed over onto the children of Ammon" (Judg. 11:29).

"And the Spirit of God came upon Saul when he heard those tidings, and his anger was kindled greatly" (1 Sam. 7:6).

"The Spirit of God hath made me, and the breath of the Almighty has given me life" (Job 33:4).

We must realistically conclude from the above scriptures that the Spirit of God was in various Old Testament characters. It is said of some in plain words that they were filled with the Spirit. We must also recognize that only a few people in Israel had this experience.

John the Baptist was born six months before Jesus. An angel told his father that John would be filled with the Holy Ghost, even from his mother's womb (Luke 1:15).

Zechariah, John's father, was filled with the Holy Ghost after John was born (Luke 1:67). Before then, John's mother was also filled with the Holy Ghost (Luke 1:41).

All the events leading up to death, burial, and resurrection of Christ took place in the Old Testament under the law. The law was observed by Jesus and the apostles as well as the new converts. They were Jews, and God dealt with them in a specific order.

Peter spoke about the "Spirit of Christ which was in them" (prophets) (1 Peter 1:11). He also stated in 2 Peter 1:21, "For the prophecy came not in old time by the will of men. But holy men spake as they were moved upon by the Holy Ghost."

## THE HOLY GHOST, OR HOLY SPIRIT IN THE NEW TESTAMENT:

"But the manifestation of the Spirit is given to every man to profit withal" (1 Cor. 12:7).

To understand the work of the Holy Ghost, we must examine Scripture and understand that the Spirit is from the Father. The Greek word for manifestation is *phanerosis*. The Holy Spirit makes healings and miracles visible; manifests prophecies, tongues, and interpretations; and even gives forth wisdom, knowledge, and discernments of various kinds.

There is no scripture teaching us that the glorified man is in the believer, but in many places, we read that God that Father is in those filled with the Holy Ghost.

"One God and Father of all, who is above all, and through all, and you all" (Eph. 4:6).

"And what agreement hath the temple of God with idols? For ye are the temple of the living God; as God hath said, I will dwell in them, and walk in them; and I will be their God, and they shall be my people" (2 Cor. 6:16).

"God is a Spirit: and they that worship him, worship him in Spirit and in truth" (John 4:24).

NOTE: God is a Spirit: *rauach, pheuma*— invisible force. The Bible states that God works on the council of His own will. At His discretion, He makes Himself visible (theophanies).

"Now the Lord is that Spirit: and where the Spirit of the Lord is, there is liberty" (2 Cor. 3:17).

"For he whom God sent speaketh the word of God: for God giveth not the Spirit by measure unto him" (John 3:34).

I pray that you have noticed thus far that the Spirit of God was given only to select few in the Old Testament but that now in the church age, New Testament, because of Christ, the Spirit is given without measure to believers.

Christ as man said, "I will pray the Father and he shall give you another comforter. And this comforter is the Spirit of truth, whom the world cannot receive...for he dwelleth with you and shall be in you" (John 14:16-17). "I will not leave you comfortless, I will come to you. At that day ye shall know that I am in my Father and ye in me and I in you" (John 7:39).

John the Baptist testified that Jesus would baptize with the Holy Ghost (Matt. 3:11).

When someone is baptized in the Holy Ghost, he or she will understand these words. Your spirit will give witness to the Lord's Spirit. Jesus Christ, being of dual nature, could say both that the Father would give another comforter and, "I will send him unto you" (John 16:7). John the apostle said, "The Holy Ghost was not yet given, because Jesus was not yet glorified" (John 7:39). Peter said, "He was put to death in the flesh and quickened (made alive) by the Spirit" (1 Peter 3:18). In the book of Acts, it says, "This Jesus hath raised up therefore being by the right hand of God exalted, and having received of the Father the promise of the Holy Ghost, he had shed forth this, which ye see and hear" (Acts 2:32-33).

By understanding that the Holy Ghost is the divinity of Christ, it is clear how Peter could say it was the Spirit that testified in the prophets. In 2 Peter 1:21, he said the Holy Ghost moved them to speak. It is very common to read in the Old Testament, "Thus saith Jehovah." Therefore, the

Spirit of Christ, the Holy Ghost, and Jehovah are the one true God. In order that we might not confuse the Spirit with another spirit, Paul declared, "Now the Lord is that Spirit" (2 Cor. 3:17).

"Now the birth of Jesus Christ was on the wise: when his mother Mary was exposed to Joseph, before they came together, she found with child of the Holy Ghost" (Matt. 1:18). In Matthew 1:20, it clearly states, "For that which is conceived in her is of the Holy Ghost." We need to understand that the Father and the Holy Spirit are the same, or else we would be like the pagan religions, believing in more than one God. The angel told Mary, "The Holy Ghost shall come upon thee, and the power of the highest shall overshadow thee: there also that holy thing which shall be born of thee, shall be called the Son of God" (Luke 1:35).

John said that this miracle by the Holy Ghost was the Word made flesh. "In the beginning was the Word, and the Word was with God, and the Word was God. The same was in the beginning with God" (John 1:1-2). "And the Word was made flesh, and dwelt among us, full of grace and truth" (John 1:14).

God was the one who said, "Destroy the temple and in three days I will rise it up" (John 2:19). The divinity of Jesus could not die, but the mortal (the Son) did die. It was not a natural death; it was divinity withdrawing from humanity. No man could take his life from Him. He laid it down Himself. Paul confirmed this in Hebrews 9:14: "How much more shall the blood of Christ, who through the eternal Spirit offered himself without spot to God, purge your conscience from dead works to serve the living God?" The Son of God overcame and sat down with His Father on His throne (notice that there is only one throne and not three) (Rev. 3:21). John saw the slain Lamb in the midst of the throne (Rev. 5:6).

In Acts 3:21, we read that the heavens must receive Him until the time of restitution of all things. The disciples saw Him after He had risen. John 20:22 says, "And when he had said this, he breathed on them, and said unto them, receive ye the Holy Ghost."

NOTE: You may ask, how many times did the disciples receive the Holy Spirit because here, the Lord breathed on them to receive the Holy

Spirit. At first, they received the Spirit when they accepted Jesus Christ as their personal Savior. The second time is through the baptism of the Holy Spirit, as promised by the Lord and confirmed by John.

Paul saw Jesus in Acts 9:5 as one born out of time (1 Cor. 15:8). But the Son's place is in heaven until He comes in the clouds of great glory. At the same time, because Christ is both God and glorified man, the divinity of Christ can be with us and in us. That is why the glorified Son can be in heaven and at the same time pour out His Spirit on believers.

Always keep in mind the following statement made by the Lord: "Think not that I am come to destroy the law, or the prophets: I am not come to destroy, but to fulfill. For verily I say unto you, till heaven and earth pass, one jot or one title shall in no wise pass from the law, till all be fulfilled" (Matt. 5:17-18).

Jesus Christ, speaking to Nicodemus, said, "Verily, verily, I say unto thee, except a man be born of the water and of the Spirit, he cannot see the kingdom of God. That which born of the flesh is flesh: and that which is born of the Spirit, is Spirit" (John 3:5-6).

"Thus it is written, and thus it is behooved Christ to suffer, and to rise from the dead the third day: and that repentance and remission of sins should be preached in his name among and all nations beginning at Jerusalem" (Luke 24:46-47).

"Go ye therefore, and teach all nations, baptizing them in the name of the Father, and the Son, and of the Holy Ghost" (Matt. 28:19).

NOTE: A.T. Robertson's *A Grammar of the Greek New Testament in the Light of Historical Research* states, "When a second article does occur, it accents on a different aspect of the (one) person or phase of the subject." I strongly feel this is correct since Isaiah 9:6,declares Yeshua is the everlasting Father. There are three manifestations—Father, Son, and Holy Ghost.

John came from the wilderness to prepare the way for Jehovah. Then who showed up? Jesus. "The voice of him that crieth in the wilderness, prepare ye the way of the LORD, Make straight in the desert a highway for our God" (Isa. 40:3), also seen in Matthew 3:3. "I indeed baptize you with water unto repentance: but he that cometh after me is mightier than I, whose shoes I am not worthy to wear: he shall baptize you with the Holy Ghost, and with fire" (Matt. 3:11).

When Jesus came to John to be baptized, Jesus said, "Suffer it to be so now: for thus it becometh us to fulfill righteousness" (Matt. 3:15).

Jesus was a Jew and well-versed in the law. It was necessary to be baptized because He knew the importance of water (water of separation, Num. 19:20). He was fulfilling His important law by being emerged in water. "And Jesus, when he was baptized, went up straight way out of the water: and lo the heavens were open unto him, and he saw the Spirit of God descending like a dove, and lightening upon him" (Matt. 3:16).

Following are the accounts of baptism of water and of the Holy Ghost: the great commission of Matthew 28:19 was a commandment for the church instituted by Jesus Christ. The apostle Peter and others understood that by invoking the name of Jesus Christ, they would be fulfilling the commandment or the great commission as it is understood by most Christians.

And suddenly there came a sound from heaven as of a rushing mighty wind, and it filled all the house in which they were sitting. And there appeared unto them cloven tongues like as of fire, and it sat upon each of them. And they were all filled with the Holy Ghost, and began to speak with other tongues, as the Spirit gave them utterance.

- Acts 2:2-4

The manifestation of being baptized (filled) in the Holy Ghost is evident by speaking in other tongues. The account states that Peter stood up with the eleven others and preached about Jesus Christ, repentance and remission of sins, and baptism in the Holy Ghost:

Then Peter said unto them, repent, and be baptized every one of you in the name of Jesus Christ for the remission of sins, and ye shall receive the gift of the Holy Ghost.

For the promise is unto you, and to your children, and to all that are far off. Even unto many as the Lord our God shall call. Then they that gladly received his word were baptized: and the same day they were added unto them about three thousand souls.

- Acts 2:38-41

Christianity today is a watered-down version. All churches today ask you to do is raise your arms and pray a so-called "sinner's prayer." The results of the message by the apostle Peter was that 3,000 souls were added to the church. This was the beginning of the congregation. This apostolic message was the foundation because all the apostles were together and in agreement. "And are all built upon the foundation of the Apostles and prophets, Jesus Christ himself being the chief cornerstone" (Eph. 2:20). Peter said again in chapter 3 verse 19, "Repent ye therefore, and be converted, that your sins be blotted out, when the times of refreshing shall come from the presence of the Lord."

"Neither is there salvation in any other: for there is none other name under heaven given among men, whereby we must be saved" (Acts 4:12).

"And when they had prayed, the place was shaken where they were assembled together: and they were all filled with the Holy Ghost, and they spake the word of God with boldness" (Acts 4:31).

In Acts chapter 8, we find Philip, the first evangelist, preaching. "Then Philip went down to the city of Samaria, and preached Christ unto them…But when they believed Philip preaching the things concerning the kingdom of God, and the name of Jesus Christ, they were baptized, both men and women" (Acts 8:5, 12). After Philip had preached unto the people of Samaria, they accepted Jesus Christ and were baptized in water but had not received the baptism of the Holy Spirit for it comes from God. "Then laid they their hands on them, and they received the Holy Ghost" (Acts 8:17).

Philip, evangelizing to an Ethiopian eunuch, said: "And as they went on their way, they came unto a certain water: and the eunuch said, see here is water; what doth hinder me to be baptized?...And he commanded the chariot to stand still: and they went down both into the water, both Philip and the eunuch; and he baptized him" (Acts 8:36, 38).

Acts chapter 9 relates the conversion of Paul:

> And Ananias went his way, and entered into the house: and putting his hands on him said, brother Saul, the Lord, even Jesus, that appeared unto thee in the way as thou camest, has sent me, that thou mightiest receive thy sight, and be filled with the Holy Ghost. And immediately there fell from his eyes as it had been scales: and he received sight forthwith, and arose, and was baptized.
>
> - Acts 9:17-18

It is important when you believe in Jesus Christ to repent and follow through with baptism of water and of Spirit.

Acts chapter 10 tells of an experience that happened when Peter went to the house of Cornelius, a Gentile. "While Peter yet spake these words, the Holy Ghost fell on all of them which heard the word. Because that on the Gentiles also was poured out of the gift of the Holy Ghost" (Acts 10:44-45). What was the manifestation or proof that the Holy Ghost was poured out on them? "For they heard them speak with tongues, and magnified God. Can any man forbid water, that these should not be baptized, which have received the Holy Ghost as well as we? And he commanded them to be baptized in the name of the Lord, (Jesus Christ)" (Acts 10:46-48). Also see Joel 2:28.

Acts chapter 19 tells of a similar experience with Paul and John's disciples:

> And it came to pass, that while Apollos was at Corinth, Paul having passes through the upper coast came to Ephesus: and finding

certain disciples. He said unto them, have ye received the Holy Ghost since ye believed? And they said unto him, we have not so much as heard whether there be any Holy Ghost. When they heard this, they were baptized in the name of the Lord Jesus. And when Paul laid his hands upon them, the Holy Ghost came on them: and they spake with tongues and prophesied.

- Acts 19:1-2, 5-6

It is a sad thing that many congregations throughout the world do not believe in the Holy Ghost in our time. In the book of Acts, we clearly see the manifestation of the Holy Spirit and how foundation of baptism of water and Spirit should be preached. For the promise is for all and as many as the Lord should call up to His second coming. The church today needs to invite the Spirit of the Lord into its assemblies in order for us to follow the pattern of the foundation set by the apostles. One interesting note is that John's disciples were baptized again in the name of the Lord Jesus Christ. There is only one baptism in water and one in the Holy Spirit. That is why the Lord said in order to enter into the kingdom of heaven, one must be baptized in water and Spirit.

# CONCLUSION

"Hear the word of the Lord, ye children of Israel: For the Lord hath a controversy with the inhabitants of the land, because there is no truth, nor mercy, nor knowledge of God in the land" (Hos. 4:2). This scripture holds as true today as when it was written to the people of Israel. Christianity today has fallen away from the true foundation set by the apostles, Christ being the true cornerstone. Many people don't take time out to search the Scriptures and decide for themselves what is true. Too many take the word of so-called apostles, prophets, teachers, or pastors.

We need to examine what is being taught. Is it biblical in truth or twisted and worded with no true foundation? The body of Christ (church) has been contaminated by too many theologians, scholars, and teachers who are not filled by the Spirit of God to teach or preach truth.

I pray that this book will awaken a sincere desire to study the Word and be ready to give an answer to every man or woman who asks as Scripture states, "Study to be approved by God" (2 Tim. 2:15).

History tells us that the Roman emperor Constantine summoned all the bishops of the church for a general council at Nicaea in the year AD 325. The principal work of this council was the settlement of a great dispute which had arisen over the nature of Christ. Athanasius of Alexandria brought forth the Trinitarian view, which the council accepted, and they formed what is known as the "Nicene Creed." Later, at the close of the first century, the emperor Theodosius made Christianity the state religion, and the organization was given the name "Catholic." The Catholic church still embraces the doctrine of the Trinity and has handed it down to us. This doctrine is also embraced by many daughter "congregations" that proceeded from the Catholic church.

For the benefit of any who may think this doctrine of the oneness of God complicated, I feel it will be helpful to give the "Doctrine of the Trinity." It appeared originally as the "Athanasius Creed." The only change made by the daughter of the Roman church was leaving out the Catholic church.

"The Doctrine of the Trinity" has been handed down in the following form:

1. Whosoever will be saved, before all things it is necessary to hold the Catholic faith.
2. Which faith except everyone do keep whole and unfiled, without doubt his shall perish everlastingly.
3. But this is the Catholic faith: that we worship one God in trinity, and trinity in unity:
4. Neither confounding the persons; nor dividing the substance.
5. For there is one person of the father; another of the son; another of the Holy Ghost

6.  But the Godhead of the Father, and of the Son, and of the Holy Ghost is all one: the glory equal. The majesty co-eternal.

7.  Such as the Father is, such is the Son, such is the Holy Ghost.

8.  The Father is uncreated; the Son is uncreated; the Holy Ghost is uncreated.

9.  The Father is incomprehensible; the Son is incomprehensible; the Holy Ghost is incomprehensible.

10. The Father is eternal; Son is eternal; the Holy Ghost is eternal.

11. And yet there are not three eternals; but one eternal.

12. And so three are not three uncreated; nor three incomprehensible, but one uncreated, and one incomprehensible.

13. So likewise the Father is almighty; the Son is almighty; and the Holy Ghost is almighty.

14. And yet there are not three almighties, but one almighty.

15. So the Father is God; the Son is God; and the Holy Ghost is God.

16. And yet three and not three Gods, but one God

17. So the Father is Lord; the Son is Lord, and the Holy Ghost is Lord.

18. And yet there are not three Lords, but one Lord.

19. For life as we are compelled by the Christian verity to acknowledge every person by himself to be God and Lord.

20. So are we also forbidden by the Catholic religion to say: there are three Gods, or three Lords.

21. The Father is made of none; neither created nor begotten

22. The Son is of the Father alone; not made, nor created; but begotten.

23. The Holy Ghost is of the Father and the Son not made; neither created; nor begotten, but proceeding.

24. Thus there is one Father, not three Fathers; one Son, not three Sons; one Holy Ghost; not three Holy Ghosts.

25. And in this trinity none is before or after another; none greater nor less than another.

26. But the whole three persons are co-eternal together, and co-equal.

27. So that in all things, as before said. The unity in trinity, and the trinity in unity is to be worshiped.
28. He therefore, that will be saved, must thus think of the trinity.

The above is taken from "The Creed of Athanasius" (Vol. 7, page 366, Anti-Nicene Fathers).

Such reasoning is absurd, and every honest person ought to recognize that this reasoning belongs only in the Catholic church with the rest of her old superstitions that aim only to keep her followers in darkness to the true teaching of the Word of God.

This creed not only contradicts the Word of God but is self-contradictory as well. There is only one true God, who has manifested Himself as Father, Son, and Holy Ghost in order to save us from our own sins that consume us. The grace of God is yours to take by faith and believe in Him who was sent as the Word.

Lightning Source UK Ltd.
Milton Keynes UK
UKHW021851161220
375343UK00008B/455